Dedicated to:

The Heathfield PageTurners
without whom,
I would never have discovered
20 word stories.

How it all began

At a recent meeting of my book club, members shared a short story they had each struggled to write. The stories had to be 20 words or less!

I hadn't written a story and therefore started jotting down some thoughts. When it was my turn to share a story, I was amazed and delighted to discover that, firstly my story sounded Ok and secondly that the other members loved what I had written. My interest in very short stories was born and I started to create this book, that evening.

Each story is complete in its own right. However, many of the stories could be the beginning, or in some cases, the end of a longer story.

How could this book be used?

This book has been created in an open format to allow you to relate to each story in your own way. I have avoided the use of illustrations to ensure that I do not impose my interpretation of the stories on you, the reader. There is plenty of space on each page for you to capture your own thoughts about the stories.

These stories would be ideal as:
- A short break from other tasks
- A discussion topic
- A distraction when stressed
- A lift when feeling down
- A way of gaining a new perspective
- A reward for completing a difficult task

Why not treat yourself to a twenty word story!

In the dim candlelight

she finally noticed it

and smiled.

Having waited so long,

she burst into tears!

The sun is up,

warming my face.

Spring is finally here.

Will it bring what

I'm hoping for?

His hat was askew,

one shoelace undone

and his trousers torn

but he was back.

Now it would be OK.

The train thundered by.

Because it hadn't stopped,

she was still free to decide

to stay or go back!

The dog barked and barked.

By morning it was silent

– exhausted.

It knew,

but didn't understand!

Hammer and nails

followed by

lots of brightly coloured paint

– the sign to

welcome him home,

was ready.

As he worked,

his body glistened

in the sun.

After all those weeks

it was finally complete.

With cobwebs across the nose,

bits of polystyrene

in his fur and

chunks missing from his ear,

Tom was back!

At last the sun rose

over the horizon,

casting a warm glow.

The new day would finally

bring closure.

Despite the mud, it rang.

He would never know

she'd dropped it.

She would never know

he'd tried.

It was to be the centerpiece

of their Christmas.

Now it was being burnt.

How did it go so wrong?

The strum of the guitar

changed tempo.

It triggered memories

of a previous life –

that seemed so far away.

The smoke twisted up

through the hole and

merged with the cold air.

It had escaped – how could I?

The waves parted.

Charlie emerged triumphant.

He staggered up the beach

knowing he would live,

to try again.

The brightly coloured scarf

billowed in the wind.

Then slowly descended

toward the lifeless body

on the beach.

The fragrance of the flower

lasted for ages.

Or could it be that

time stood still,

while he remembered?

Charlie went to bed.

The world moved on

but he didn't.

The world missed out.

His idea was brilliant.

The lights appeared

through the fog.

They were so nearly home

and safe.

Or were they?

With a luxurious stretch

and a lightening pounce,

dinner was ready!

John so wanted it to happen.

He wasn't surprised

when it did.

However it wasn't quite

what he'd expected!

She swerved round the corner

and screeched to a holt.

The drive was empty.

Thankfully

she'd got there first!

Claire jumped up

and flagged down the bus.

She had finally found

the courage to leave

and start again.

The door closed silently

behind me.

I had no idea

where the road ahead

was taking me!

He knew he'd

got it badly wrong.

But would he have the strength

to put it right?

He opened his eyes

and watched me

– then sprang.

The door crashed shut.

I was safe– for now.

The rose bloomed

for the first time

in many years.

I knew this was

the new beginning

I craved.

There was a squeal of brakes,

followed by a loud crunch.

Then silence.

John wouldn't be home

for tea.

The last leaf dropped

and the tree was bare.

He knew that she would stay

until the snowdrops arrived.

Lisa gazed into his eyes

in wonder,

as the bullet ripped

through her body.

He knew his secret was safe –

for now.

The anticipation built for weeks.

Finally the invitations went out.

He already knew,

that his would never arrive.

The last petal dropped.

The flower that had

symbolised hope for so long,

meant that Peter

could finally move on!

His last breathe gently subsided.

The lights grew brighter

and a far more

exciting existence began.

The relentless icy water

cascaded over him.

It cleared his mind.

Only then did he realise

what he'd done.

The lottery numbers matched.

They should have brought

excitement and joy.

Instead they only

intensified the pain.

Finally she heard the sound

she had been waiting for.

The engine died.

He would make it— just!

The bullet whistled past.

He would live.

However, it would be a long time

before he could forget!

She wandered through

the waves of lavender

and savoured the evening air.

Jane knew that soon

she would be free.

In their sheltered corner,

the flowers bloomed

and then died.

How long would what they hid

remain secret?

She left the traffic behind

and headed north.

It would be years

before she knew

if her decision was right.

The lights flashed on.

As the gates shut behind her

she knew she had made it.

But was she safe?

The road lay straight ahead

in the blistering heat.

Unknown to Claire

so did her future happiness.

Ping.

Ebay advised that it was sold.

Finally there was closure

and now she could move on.

The guests were leaving.

The excitement of the day subsided.

She already knew she had made a big mistake.

With a gentle rock

and a loud crack

a tiny beak appeared.

Mum already knew that

this one was special.

Engaged again and again.

Time was running out.

Without help

he wasn't going to make it,

this time.

Claude really, really wanted it.

He knew it wasn't allowed.

But would anyone

even notice?

The car hiccupped and died.

She had no choice.

She got out and finally faced

what she'd hoped to avoid.

The redial button pinged again

– engaged.

He couldn't give up

so he tried again and again.

They laughed at him

as he tried to move forward.

They knew what awaited him.

Unfortunately he didn't.

The barren ground broke open

and a small green shoot appeared.

Despite everything,

life would continue after all.

The thunder of hooves

triggered the fear once more.

As the full horror gripped him,

he knew he had lost.

He picked up the delicate necklace

and clipped it around her neck.

She knew that now

her freedom was over.

The door opened

and they emerged smiling.

Would their current happiness

be enough?

The rain fell in sheets

across the hillside.

Two small faces appeared briefly

at the window,

then disappeared forever.

He was so far behind.

Would he ever make it?

Then suddenly the clouds lifted.

He discovered he'd arrived.

The trickle became a roar.

When the dust settled,

it was so much better

than she had ever imagined.

The tears rolled down her cheeks

as the teeth finally sprang open.

It had let her go!

The bell rang and

the door sprang open.

I was living my ultimate fantasy

– they had arrived!

Another day

and another new strategy.

Only 10 more attempts

were allowed.

Will it ever open?

8, 6, 4, 2

and he'd got it.

The family would be shocked

but did they really need to know?

The boom across the water

echoed through the fog.

Now we knew where we were

– will we ever get back?

We had finally arrived.

When I opened the boot,

out popped a furry head.

Thomas had decided to join us!

Another day, another bill.

Would it ever end?

Then there it was

small and sparkly –

just when I needed it!

The rough sea

threw him onto the beach.

As the water receded

he knew he would survive.

The purring engine died.

She stretched and

opened her eyes –

then panicked.

Why are we here?

The persistent hum of the pedals

kept me moving forward.

I wondered where I would be

by dawn?

The daffodils wilted and died.

Spring was over.

Summer was far too frightening

to contemplate!

It tickled my nose.

When I woke up

it was in front of me.

Yipee – I knew I'd be rich!

Have a go at writing your own

twenty-word story.

You might be surprised

at what you come up with!

If you're pleased with your work,
why not enter my competition for the
best twenty-word story of the year.
A prize will be awarded in Dec 2016
Email your stories to me at
E:barbara@barbarahibbartcoaching.co.uk

About the Author

Barbara lives with her husband and daughter in Heathfield, East Sussex. She is a business coach and works with people to help them create change in their business and personal lives. Barbara also loves cats, pottering in the garden, cooking for friends and the sea.

Future Books

Look out for future books by Barbara

including :

Twenty-word stories for children

The Wheel of Life

A childrens' story with a twist!

www.barbarahibbartcoaching.co.uk

Printed in Great Britain
by Amazon